in black

volume iii of a silent trilogy

by

sparling

© 2025 Simon Darling
All rights reserved.

No part of this publication may be reproduced, stored in a retrieval system, or transmitted in any form or by any means—electronic, mechanical, photocopying, recording, or otherwise—without the prior written permission of the publisher.

Published by **Untold Imprint**
www.sdarling-art.com

ISBN: 978-1-7641672-2-2
Printed in: Australia

THIS IS A WORK OF POETRY AND PHILOSOPHY. ANY RESEMBLANCE TO REAL PERSONS, LIVING OR DEAD, IS PURELY COINCIDENTAL.

*a minute of surrender buried in the
quiet nothing we became*

this is a collection of moments
gathered from the furthest edges of the in-between—
some formed in clarity,
others carved from the dark
where thought dissolves
and meaning loses its shape.
not in order,
not in narrative,
but as fragments
shaped by silence,
absence,
and surrender.
in black is the last of three.
this is not a story.
it is the quiet after the final thought.
you are not asked to interpret it.
only to sit inside its hush,
and feel what remains.
this is not just a book.
it is an ending,
meant to be absorbed,
not explained.

i. beyond

i. beyond

darkness spreads
swiftly these days;
in the death
of the night
i have these dreams,
taking me
to the dark side
of the moon,
where autumn
flowers bloom.

i. beyond

in the sublime solitude at the world's demise,
i stood amidst the remnants of fractured beauty,
where echoes of silence painted a melancholic masterpiece,
and the fading sun cast a haunting glow
over the elegy of a solitary existence.

i. beyond

feeling nothing
is also
a feeling—
a soft vanishing
the mind mistakes
for peace.

i. beyond

an unknown mystery,
sealed in a quiet gaze—
a shattered mind
with a burden
to bear.

within
solitude's grasp,
it slowly
diminishes;

it's the sorrowful tale
of beloved
replications.

i. beyond

beyond the edges of thought,
a faint vibration waits—
a place where reason blurs
and something older
pulls you forward.
you step into it
without knowing
if you'll return.

i. beyond

meet me at the spot where the world unwinds,
a rendezvous on the precipice of an era's demise.

as shadows elongate
and echoes of existence wane,
in this cosmic twilight
where conclusions are drawn.

at the spot where the final chapter is etched,
we stand, witnesses to a world in its last breath.
the skyline—
once a tapestry of dreams and endeavours—
now dissolves into the cosmic stream,
timeless and vast.

here, where time converges
and memories coalesce,
meet me at the spot
where futures unravel and compress.

in the hush of this celestial dusk,
whispers of what was
echo through the cosmic corridor,
a nostalgic buzz.

at the spot,
the meeting point of dusk and infinity,
we share the silence—
an unspoken affinity.

as the world concludes its journey,
folding into lore,
our presence lingers,
a testament to what came before.

meet me at the spot
where the cosmic winds entwine—
a farewell to the known,
an embrace of the divine.

in this meeting place,
where the world finds its end,
we stand, united,
as the cosmic curtains descend.

i. beyond

in the depths
of nightfall,
where shades
conspire,
a chilling silence
wraps around
us all.

the moon,
a pale spectator,
casts a peculiar
glow upon the world,

revealing
the ominous enigmas
that lie below
the cover
of an odd shimmer.

the moon's
eerie gaze,
a cryptic sphere,

unraveling
riddles
hidden in pain,

a response
of secrets,
a silent cry,

in this
paradox's
embrace,
we find our decline.

i. beyond

seated at the edge of the world,
watching the stars as they burn out
in the cosmic descent.

the world, in its final throes,
whispers secrets in the breeze;
i, an observer in the cosmic theatre,
witness the celestial tease.

the horizon stretches into the abyss—
an endless canvas. stars, once luminous storytellers,
dimming in celestial distress.

at the precipice of existence,
where time unravels its final thread,
i sit, a witness to the cosmic unravelling,
the imminent spread.

in the quiet expanse, where echoes of existence wane,
i ponder the mysteries of life—
the joys, the sorrows, the pain.

the stars, like embers,
flicker in a cosmic requiem,
as the world reaches its finale—
a celestial hymn.

the cosmic winds carry
the symphony of goodbyes,
a silent lamentation as constellations fade in the skies.

seated at the edge,
i become part of the cosmic narrative,
a participant in the cosmic dance,
as the world becomes elusive.

in this mysterious twilight,
where worlds collide, i watch the stars burn out
in the cosmic tide.

at the edge of the world,
an observer in the cosmic play—
as the universe concludes,
in silence, i remain.

i. beyond

there is a line
no one admits crossing—
thin as breath,
soft as a fading dream.
yet once you pass it,
the world tilts,
and everything familiar
leans away from you.

i. beyond

even the longest days
collapse eventually—
their light thinning
into a silence
that feels like it's waiting
for something to break

memories linger there,
but not as they were;
they distort in the dim,
slipping into shapes
I don't fully recognise,
yet somehow know too well

they return
when the world goes quiet,
uninvited,
heavy with all the things
I thought I'd survived

and when the last flicker fades,
what remains
is not the day
nor the truth of it—
only the shadow it leaves behind,
the part that follows,
even when I swear
I've already walked beyond it.

i. beyond

in the fading hours of time's relentless march,
we glimpse the spectre of better days, a haunting arch.
as the shadows deepen and the darkness swells,
memories of brighter moments sink in sorrowful wells.

at the end of time, where echoes of laughter fade,
we mourn the lost brilliance—
a melancholic cascade.
in the abyss of oblivion, where hope wanes thin,
we ponder the fleeting glimpse
of what could have been.

i. beyond

beyond the spoken
lies the truer language—
an ache,
a shadow,
a pulse that answers
questions you didn't know
you were asking.
you listen,
even when it hurts.

i. beyond

in the realm where shadows wear
silhouette disguise,
she was her own
in an unusual way.

her hair,
a flow of midnight haze—
a mysterious aura,
a surreal twist.

eyes like galaxies,
galactic and profound;
in the universe of daydreams,
she takes a leap.

her laughter,
a melody of unusual notes,
echoing through
dreamlike, psychedelic spheres.

she spins
in echoes
of irregular poise—
a strange ballet
in a fantastical space.

her thoughts,
constellations
in a weirdly shaped twirl—
she is a mystery,
an imaginary paradox.

from her voice,
stardust and whispers
collide—
a strange girl
in a creative stride.

in the strangeness
of existence,
she's an unlikely twist—
a peculiar poem
written in an average sphere,
where time stops
until she disappears.

i. beyond

beneath the obsidian sky,
a moon made of fractured dreams
cast its eerie glow over a forest
where shadows whispered secrets
to the twisted trees.

i. beyond

midnight moons rise on dark wings, their ascent shrouded in
mystery; silhouettes drift against a tapestry
woven of deep indigo and black.

each phase a whisper, each crater a secret kept from the sun's
blinding light. in their silent arc, they pull at the seams
of the sea and the soul alike—
a force felt in the marrow, in the ebb and flow of nocturnal
tides.

the night air grows thick with the scent of unseen blooms,
awakening to the touch of pale beams
that traverse vast and distant spaces;
their ghostly illumination casting shadows
where none should fall creating realms of half-things, half-
thoughts, dwelling at the edge of sight.

trees bend subtly, as if to speak;
leaves rustle with the weight of untold stories.
beneath these dark-winged moons,
paths appear less trodden, more winding,
drawing the wakeful to wander—
pulled by a curiosity tugging at the corners of the conscious
mind.

what hands have framed this moonlit spectacle,
what whispers guide its steady climb—
each night a new enigma painted in the old, cold light?

what secrets live in this lunar glow,
where shadows bloom and retreat like tides—
each ebb a pulling back of the world's curtain,
revealing glimpses not meant for human eyes?

the world under this moonlight
dances quietly on the brink of revelation;
every creature moves as if aware of eyes upon it,
each step a note in a silent melody
played beneath the dome of heaven's watchful gaze.

thus do midnight moons rise—
on wings unseen but deeply felt,
guiding the night with hidden hands,
cloaked in the quiet beauty
of dark mysteries.

i. beyond

i walked past the last certainty,
out where the air
grew strangely still.
the sky bent inward,
the ground unthreaded—
and in that unraveling,
i understood
how small i'd been.

i. beyond

in the grand finale of life's intricate play,
the end unfolds with an ironic display.
as curtains draw close on the stage of fate,
irony reigns supreme,
sealing our ultimate state.

i. beyond

i am only an invention of darkness,
a fleeting shadow cast upon the canvas of existence—
a whisper in the night, soon to fade into silence,
a figment of imagination destined to vanish with the dawn.

in the depths of the night, i find solace;
for it is in darkness that i find my truth
and embrace the depths of my own being,
free from the harsh light of day.

but with the first light of dawn, i will vanish—
a ghost in the morning mist, fading into the ether,
leaving behind only echoes of my presence,
a memory in the minds of those who knew me.

and yet, in my transient existence,
i find a strange comfort;
for it is in the impermanence of life
that i find meaning and purpose.

for though i may be only an invention of darkness,
i am also a reminder of the fleeting nature of existence
and the beauty of embracing the present moment
before it too fades
into the past.

i. beyond

in the desolate beauty of the world's end,
solitary shadows stretched across a kaleidoscope
of abandoned landscapes, where the only company
was the vivid decay of once vibrant colours,
painting a poignant canvas of loneliness
in the dying light.

i. beyond

beyond the quiet
is a deeper quiet—
the kind that swallows
names, memories, time.
yet in that void,
something stirs,
a whisper of a world
not meant for the living.

ii. become

ii. become

in the quiet chaos of my mind,
you appeared in my reflection;
i held onto that image,
and it burned its way
through the years.

ii. become

to become is to loosen
the grip of who you were—
to watch the old self
fracture quietly,
falling away in pieces
you no longer claim.
change rarely announces itself;
it just begins.

ii. become

i became someone else
slowly—
like light fading from a room
you didn't notice dimming.
one day i looked inward
and the shape of me
was unfamiliar,
yet stubbornly mine.

ii. become

the past resembles
a place of reference,
where we should not reside—
but endlessly creating
ourselves,
we'll do all that
just to become
strangers again.

ii. become

becoming is a kind of burning—
not fire,
but an inner heat
that melts what no longer fits.
i step out of myself
carrying only the parts
that survived
the quiet blaze.

ii. become

i felt the shift
long before i named it—
a soft distortion
beneath the ribs,
a slow undoing
of the person you pretended to be.
in that breaking,
i finally knew.

ii. become

in the tapestry of existence, our touch leaves a stain;
as humans, we ruin everything, including each other, in vain.
fragile hearts bear scars of our relentless sway,
in the dark and sentimental dance where shadows play.

our hands, once tender, now wield a callous grip,
leaving trails of devastation in our reckless trip.
we bruise souls in the pursuit of fleeting gain;
as humans, we ruin everything—leaving behind a bane.

in the echo chamber of our deeds, regrets softly sigh,
as we realize the cost of our actions in the silent cry.
each interaction tainted by our flawed touch;
in the lament of human frailty, we find little as such.

ii. become

to become anything
i first had to break—
quietly,
without spectacle,
like glass cracking under frost.
only then
could the pieces decide
their new arrangement.

ii. become

becoming is not rising—
it is descending first,
into the parts of yourself
you tried to bury.
only after the fall
does the shape return,
stranger, sharper,
yet somehow truer.

ii. become

we break bonds with the weight of our desires,
leaving behind a trail of smouldering fires.
in the dark corners where sentiments smother,
as humans, we ruin everything, including one another.

ii. become

maybe forever was a word meant for memories
and not for the fragile hearts of people;
for in the tapestry of time, we are but fleeting threads,
woven together only to unravel in the end.

we cling to the illusion of eternity
in the embrace of fleeting moments,
but like sand slipping through clenched fists,
forever eludes our grasp,
slipping away.

in the quiet corners of our souls, we mourn
for the dreams we dared to believe in;
but reality is a harsh mistress—unforgiving,
reminding us that nothing lasts forever.

and so we are left to wander in the wreckage
of promises whispered but never kept,
as the echoes of our hopes fade into the abyss,
lost amidst the ruins
of what could have been.

ii. become

i shed versions of myself
the way night sheds its shadows
at the first warning of dawn.
what remains
is not new—
just revealed,
finally brave enough
to be seen.

ii. become

i did not notice the moment
i changed—
only the aftermath,
the subtle ache
of having outgrown
my own reflection.
to become
is to leave behind
what once felt permanent.

ii. become

white blank paper—
as i recognize the beauty of simplicity,
i feel the urge to destroy that beauty
with words of destruction.

in the pristine emptiness,
i see potential—endless possibilities
waiting to be unleashed;
but instead of creation,
i feel the pull of destruction,
the desire to mar the purity
with the chaos of existence.

there's a darkness within me, a longing
to defile the innocence with the weight of my pain,
to stain the blankness with the ink of my sorrow
and watch the beauty crumble
beneath the weight of my words.

but even as i yield to the impulse,
there's a sadness, a regret;
for in the act of destruction,
i lose something precious—
something pure.

and yet, there is a release, a catharsis,
as i give voice to the turmoil within
and watch the darkness spill onto the page—
a testament to the complexity
of human emotion.

ii. become

so let the ink flow,
let the words spill;
for in the destruction of beauty
there is also a kind of creation—
a transformation, a rebirth
that speaks to the depths
of the human soul.

iii. between

iii. between

a brief
sudden
disconnected
f e e l i n g
from the illusion
of one's own
thoughts.

iii. between

between who i was
and who i might become,
there is a narrow corridor
where nothing fits—
not memory,
not desire,
not the ghost of who i tried to be.
i walk it anyway.

iii. between

in the shadowed hours when reality unravels,
we only talk about real shit when we're fucked up.
the veneer of pretence crumbles with every sip,
as intoxication unveils the truths we keep.

sober tongues may dance in cautious circumspect,
but in the realm of inebriation, honesty takes effect.
the blurred lines of sobriety reveal candid confessions—
fucked up, we find refuge in genuine expressions.

the night becomes a confessional, a sanctuary profound,
where unspoken realities echo in the background.
in the embrace of altered states, truths intertwine;
we only talk about real shit when we're in that line.

iii. between

caught between endings,
i hover—
not falling,
not rising,
just held in the stillness
where time forgets to move.
here, even my shadow
hesitates to follow.

iii. between

gloomy obscurities
appear
from the emptiness
of reality,

a secret world
found
in an unseen
place.

here you
ought to
whisper,

almost as silent
as the blink
of your eye.

silent questions
turned bad,

in the depths
of the night
we never
had.

iii. between

"don't pretend to miss me when i'm gone,"
echoes linger in the silent dawn.
words spoken, bitter, cutting like a knife,
leaving scars upon the tapestry of life.

empty promises, now shattered, lie
in the remnants of a fading sky.
for when absence falls, true feelings are shown—
don't cloak deceit in echoes all alone.

iii. between

between one heartbeat and the next,
a question opens—
quiet, sharp,
a small tear in the fabric
of what i believe.
i look into it,
but the answer
never forms a shape.

iii. between

in the quiet hours of slumber's embrace,
i drift away to a forbidden place—
where fantasies roam, unbridled and free,
and the taste of her lingers, enticing me.

in dreams, her lips part in a silent sigh
as i trace the curve where her secrets lie.
her taste becomes a symphony of sweet desire,
igniting flames that dance with fervent fire.

each breath a whisper, a tantalizing tease,
as i explore the depths of her mysteries.
her essence floods my senses, rich and bold;
in the realm of dreams, our passion unfolds.

and when morning breaks, i wake with a sigh,
yet the memory of her taste still lingers nigh.
for in the realm of dreams, she's mine to savour—
the taste of her lips,
a lingering flavour.

iii. between

between who i was
and who i might become,
there is a narrow corridor
where nothing fits.
i linger there—
half-formed, half-forgotten,
waiting for a door
that may never open.

iii. between

i exist between meanings,
where words fracture
before reaching the tongue—
where silence becomes
its own language
and everything i feel
is only half-alive,
half-known.

iii. between

i wish we met before they convinced you love is war—
before the battle lines were drawn
and scars became badges;
before hearts were armoured
and trust barricaded
in the fortress of cynicism
where vulnerability is a weakness.

but now, we stand on opposite sides of the divide,
strangers in a world where love is a battlefield,
caught in the crossfire of our own insecurities
and the echoes of past wounds
that refuse to heal.

i wonder what might have been
if we had met in a time
before disillusionment set in—
before the cynics whispered their poison
and tarnished the purity of our dreams.

would we have found solace
in each other's arms,
or would we have been casualties
in the war that rages within us—
a conflict of heart and mind,
where love becomes a casualty
of our own making?

i wish we met
before they convinced you love is war—
before we became casualties
in the battle for affection
and lost ourselves in the fray,
leaving behind only the echoes
of what could have been.

iii. between

i live in the pause
between impulse and regret,
a thin strip of time
where everything feels possible
and nothing feels real.
in that trembling space,
i almost recognise myself.

iii. between

somewhere between staying
and leaving,
i lose the last piece
of what anchored me.
the world tilts,
subtle but irreversible,
and suddenly
i am between everything—
and nothing.

iii. between

a meaningless conversation in a familiar scenery,
words drift like leaves in the autumn breeze,
lost in the echoes of forgotten dreams
and the quiet hum of the everyday routine.

we speak in circles, dancing around the truth,
as the scenery fades into the background noise
and the weight of our words hangs heavy in the air—
a tangible reminder of our disconnect.

but still, we press on, pretending to listen,
as the minutes tick by like grains of sand,
caught in the hourglass of our own making,
trapped in the cycle of meaningless exchange.

in the familiar scenery of our shared existence,
we find ourselves adrift in a sea of sameness,
lost in the monotony of our own making,
yearning for something more, yet unsure of what.

and so we continue on in this dance of absurdity,
hoping for meaning in the meaningless,
but finding only emptiness in the echoes
of a conversation that never was.

iii. between

between the silence
and the word unspoken,
something fragile stirs—
a thought not yet born,
a truth not yet willing.
i hold it gently,
afraid that naming it
will make it disappear.

iii. between

is it my fault that you're lost,
or yours, that i remain?
in this dark, mysterious expanse,
we linger—
both seeking, both haunted
by the same relentless question
the night refuses to answer.

iv. beneath

iv. beneath

within the pain
of memories,
the past
will attack
the present.

iv. beneath

beneath the surface
the truth vibrates—
too fragile for daylight,
too heavy for silence.
i feel it shifting slowly,
like something buried
trying to breathe again.

iv. beneath

in such a soft focus,
the luminous shade
of reality fades away
in my mind.

i have scars
from others—
so what are
a few more from you,

although i see
the pain
in your eyes,
so similar to mine.

same desire
for belonging;
i'm used
to those empty words.

that's why
i always wait
for nightfall;
the moon never lets me go.

i believe
in the victory
of love,
because i grew up
in the sight of its downfall.

take me away
from this rush;
everything feels distorted.

i dreamt of you
before the fears
of doubt.

i wished it never
had to change—
you went so far...

away.

iv. beneath

a lot of things
don't hurt
anymore,

but nothing burns
like her cold.

i was fine
before
it began.

i am holding on
to a dream
while watching
these walls
fall down.

iv. beneath

we are lost
in the echoes
of a whispered
farewell,

we ache
in silence,
beneath
heaven's
sigh,

we are
the shadowy
corners
of our soul's
regret,

our mystery
and sadness,
which it
will forever
affect.

iv. beneath

there is a weight beneath my ribs,
a quiet stone
formed from all the words
i never said.
some nights it feels alive,
turning in the dark,
reminding me
what i chose to keep hidden.

iv. beneath

i hope
these words
will scorch
your tongue,

i hope
my ardour
will burn
your mind,

and this poem
impales
your soul—

i hope
you sense
what i felt
leaving...

iv. beneath

beneath the calm
a fracture waits—
a thin line
running through everything i hold.
i pretend not to see it,
but in still moments
i feel the world
splitting gently at its seam.

iv. beneath

buried beneath memory's ruin,
something soft still moves—
a pulse, faint and unsure,
reaching for a world
that left it behind.
i wonder if it's hope,
or just the echo
of something i lost.

iv. beneath

eyes that've
seen too much
would go blind
for this touch,

and through
whispers,
my words
will reach you.

iv. beneath

witness the scene, lost, submerged in the depths,
another chilling morning in copenhagen's solitary grip.

i yearn to guide you through these cobblestone streets,
yet, alone i traverse, wishing to bring you home.

you, indifferent to my yearning—
a harsh reality, girl,
i'm grappling to grasp
the threads of your affection.

attempting to feel the warmth of your love,
yet, i'm not fucked enough
to warrant your attention.

a fracture in the mirror,
an ominous alteration—
anticipating a shift in the reflection,
a transformation.

the image, once held,
is bound to rearrange,
evoking uncertain sentiments
as this chapter concludes.

iv. beneath

deep beneath the noise,
where thoughts fall silent,
i find the part of me
that refuses to rise.
it stays hidden,
rooted in the dark,
a reminder that not everything
was meant to be brought back to light.

iv. beneath

in the quiet chambers of solitude, a truth unfolds—
no beautiful tapestry to weave, no tales to be told.
loneliness, a silent spectre without a poetic guise,
no elegant prose to soften the ache in quiet sighs.

no majestic sunset to cloak the emptiness within,
just the stark truth, a solitary path i'm in.
loneliness—an unspoken narrative with no scenic art,
no beautiful way to explain the quiet breaking apart.

in the shadows where silence and solitude entwine,
no enchanting verses to make the loneliness benign.
no moonlit night to romanticize the soul's plea—
just the stark admission of a quiet, lonely sea.

iv. beneath

in the recesses of my mind, shadows reside—
a labyrinth of darkness where thoughts collide.
my head, a cavernous expanse, an abyss profound,
where echoes of turmoil linger
and in silence resound.

iv. beneath

it is not hell, if you like how it burns—
a paradox of pleasure in the midst of pain.
each flame licking at the edges of sanity,
leaving scars upon the soul, unseen but felt.

the heat becomes a cruel comfort
within the cold embrace,
drawing me closer to the inferno within,
where desires smolder in the ashes of regret
and the echoes of lost dreams reverberate.

in this crucible of contradiction, i dwell,
finding solace in the agony of existence—
for it is not hell, if you like how it burns,
a bittersweet embrace in the abyss of despair.

iv. beneath

in the abyss of emptiness, i wander—
a soul adrift, lost in silent ponder.
how deep can i sink into nothingness's call,
where echoes whisper in the void's thrall?

each step i take becomes a descent into the unknown,
an endless chasm where shadows are sown.
into the depths, where darkness reigns supreme,
i wonder if this is real,
or only a dream.

can i dissolve into the void's embrace,
lose myself in its cold, empty space?
in the silence, i search for a sign,
but find only the echo
of my own decline.

iv. beneath

i admit i still fantasize about you;
if you think i'm writing about you, i am—
a confession veiled in the shadows' embrace,
whispered beneath the moon's soft silver light.

in the chambers of my heart, you linger,
a ghostly presence haunting every thought;
a mystery unsolved, a riddle unsaid,
an enigma wrapped in layers of desire.

do you feel the echoes of my longing
as they drift along the edges of your dreams?
do you sense the pull of unseen forces
drawing us together across the void?

for in these words, a quiet invitation
lies hidden—waiting for your touch to find
the secret door that leads into my soul,
where mysteries and passions intertwine.

iv. beneath

in the quiet realm where shadows softly linger,
i still see the echoes of our love, my heart a stinger.
the room, a silent witness to love's quiet bloom—
yet shadows dance, and i can't reclaim the love i gave you.

the walls resonate with the hushed memories we shared,
a love once vibrant, now a melody tattered and bared.
in the soft glow of moonlight, shadows softly loom,
a poignant reminder: i can't take back the love i gave you.

the echoes of laughter, whispers of affection,
reside in the corners, a haunting reflection.
in the silent space where once our dreams did zoom,
i grapple with the truth: i can't retrieve the love i gave you.

through the dim-lit hours, in the quiet's sweet embrace,
i navigate the shadows, tracing love's fragile grace.
in this room, where memories silently consume,
i reckon with the fact: i can't undo the love i gave you.

iv. beneath

in the arsenal of the heart, memories merge—
a weapon forged from fragments of a dark recess.
the past becomes a blade, with sentiments for its edge;
a dual-purpose weapon, sharpened by a silent pledge.

in the quietude, emotions metamorphose into a storm,
and as i wield the weapon of memories, sentiments take form.
each recollection becomes a dagger, a bittersweet knife,
turned inward in the somber pursuit of navigating life.

the echoes of yesteryears rise in a haunting refrain,
as i brandish my past, using it to inflict pain.
sentiments sharpened, memories turned into a dart—
a dark and sentimental weapon, wielded from the heart.

in this battlefield of emotion, where shadows linger,
i navigate the past, a relentless emotional trigger.
a weapon forged in the crucible of time—
my memories become the verses of a melancholic rhyme.

iv. beneath

how can emptiness be so heavy—
a weight that crushes the spirit beneath its burden?
each breath becomes a struggle against the suffocating void
that consumes the soul in its relentless grasp.

in the hollow chambers of the heart, echoes linger,
whispers of longing and loss reverberating
as the emptiness expands, filling every crevice,
leaving no room for solace or sanctuary.

i carry this burden like a leaden cloak,
dragging me down into the depths of despair—
each step a weary march through the wasteland
of shattered dreams and broken promises.

and yet, in the depths of this desolation,
i find a strange comfort in the heaviness—
a reminder of the depth of my sorrow
and the weight of all that i have lost.

v. blur

v. blur

everything's absent,
but nothing left
shadowing the
f e e l i n g,
no one's feeling.

and then there was
somewhat
something
for a while...

then there was
nothing again—
unfounded
in the form
of a
f e e l i n g

v. blur

in the end
there is no revelation—
only the soft collapse
of everything we carried.
and in that quiet falling,
we understand:
we were never meant
to stay.

v. blur

in the fogged corners of my mind, emotions blurred,
shapes dissolving before i could name them.
feelings rose like half-formed shadows,
uncertain, trembling, never fully real.

love flickered in fragments, stitched with sorrow,
a pulse slipping in and out of focus.
joy and grief drifted together in the haze,
indistinguishable in their slow unravel.

each moment swayed like a distorted reflection,
until even the memory of feeling
began to fade.

in the soft collapse of everything once certain,
the last trace of emotion exhaled itself—
a quiet surrender into the blur.

v. blur

when the last shape fades,
and even memory loosens its grip,
there is a moment—
brief, breathless—
where the self lets go of itself.
in that unmaking,
something almost like peace
finally arrives.

v. blur

in the shadows, a soul entangled with the unknown,
romanticizing the uncomfortable—an odd, peculiar throne.
the unfamiliar becomes a tapestry of strange allure,
woven in the darkest corners, where discomforts endure.

they find beauty in the eerie, in the unsettling;
a dance with the shadows, where mysteries are compelling.
the whispers of the unknown drift in a haunting serenade,
in discomfort's quiet embrace, an unconventional crusade.

in uncharted territories, where unspoken fears reside,
they weave tales of the bizarre, with shadows as their guide.
romanticizing the discomfort—an intimate, twisted affair,
finding solace in the weirdness, an unlikely kind of welfare.

the uneasy silence becomes a symphony they adore,
as they wander through realms most others ignore.
in the dark and the strange, they carve out a home—
a sanctuary built where the unfamiliar has grown.

v. blur

here, at the very edge
where all things blur into one,
the truth reveals itself
not as light,
but as release.
nothing to hold,
nothing to haunt—
only the final silence
that chooses us all.

v. blur

for in the depths of the twisted mind's terrain,
i find a beauty both surreal and arcane.
the words become a dance of shadows in the night—
echoes of madness,
yet somehow right.

in the chaos of my thoughts,
i find a home,
where emotions bloom
and fears freely roam.
for those who speak with twisted minds' delight
illuminate the darkness
with their strange light.

v. blur

in the blur between ending and leaving,
i feel myself thinning—
a silhouette without a centre,
a pulse without a body.
i reach for something solid,
but even my own shadow
steps away from me.

v. blur

they call me a dreamer,
but i'm the only one who doesn't sleep—
haunted by visions that linger
in the shadows of my restless mind,
where reality fades
into the mist of forgotten wishes.

each night, i wander the corridors of my thoughts,
chasing ghosts of what could have been,
but finding only echoes of shattered dreams
whispering secrets i dare not hear.

i am a prisoner of my own imagination,
trapped in a labyrinth of endless possibility,
yet unable to find the path to salvation—
lost in the darkness of my own creation.

they call me a dreamer,
but i am a wanderer,
drifting through the void of my own making,
searching for meaning in the chaos of existence,
but finding only
the emptiness of solitude.

v. blur

sometimes i don't know how to feel,
and then it happens again—
the feeling of nothing, a void that swallows me whole,
leaving me adrift in the vast expanse of emptiness
where emotions fade into the background
like distant echoes.

in the silence of my own confusion, i search for meaning,
but find only the echo of my own uncertainty—
a haunting reminder of the fragility of existence
and the fleeting nature of human emotion.

i am a stranger in my own skin,
lost in the labyrinth of my thoughts,
where reality bends and distorts
like a funhouse mirror,
and the line between perception and illusion blurs,
leaving me questioning
the very nature of my own existence.

but still, i press on,
navigating the maze of my mind,
hoping to find some semblance of clarity
in the chaos of my own confusion
and the strange dance of nothingness
that surrounds me.

v. blur

time folds strangely here—
moments overlap,
faces echo,
meanings repeat until they're hollow.
in this place,
nothing breaks,
but nothing remains whole.
i only know i'm fading
because nothing around me notices.

v. blur

when the nights change,
so do my nightmares too—
a cryptic shift that whispers secrets dark,
unravelling the threads of sanity
in the shadowed corners of my mind.

what spectres haunt the depths
of sleep's domain?
what phantoms move through tangled webs
of dreams, where reality and illusion
twist into a surreal, trembling dance?

as the moon casts its silver spell,
the veil between the seen and unseen
grows thin; whispers from the other side
slip through like tendrils of mist
uncoiling in the night.

do my nightmares hold the key
to truths long buried,
or are they echoes of unfounded fear—
shadows cast by doubt,
flickering at the edges of sleep?

in the shifting sands of slumber,
the answers elude me,
slipping through my grasp
like a handful of fading sand.

v. blur

lost in nowhere,
a void without light,
where shadows twist
and the wind cannot speak.

the earth beneath crumbles,
unseen, unheard,
and time slips away
like dust in the air.

in this endless abyss,
i stand alone—
a fleeting echo,
swallowed by silence.

v. blur

i watch my reflection flicker,
slipping out of sync
with the person i think i am.
even mirrors forget me now,
their surface swallowing
every attempt to return
to whatever i once was.

v. blur

in the shadows of perception, disquiet descends—
episodes of derealisation, where reality bends.
the world becomes a fleeting mirage, surreal and strange,
as if life itself slips into a momentary, elusive change.

a disconnect from the tangible, from everything known;
the familiar shifts, morphing into an unfamiliar zone.
colours lose their vibrancy, sounds fade to distant echoes—
in the realm of derealisation, a quiet confusion grows.

faces once familiar wear a spectral, hollow guise,
as if seen through a lens woven from distorted lies.
emotions hover in a suspended, unreal dimension,
a disconcerting dance shaped by the mind's intention.

episodes unfold like chapters in a dissonant tale,
the ground beneath turning into an unsteady, shifting trail.
in the echo chamber of derealisation's sway,
reality becomes a transient, elusive display.

v. blur

a meaningless conversation in a familiar scenery
that no longer feels familiar,
where words drift like dust in distorted light,
clinging to the corners of our minds
like cobwebs we don't remember weaving.

the room tilts slightly,
as if reality glitches beneath our feet,
and the backdrop of our shared history
flickers between what was
and what we only think we recall.

we speak in loops,
the same phrases dissolving as soon as they're spoken—
syllables blurring into static,
their meaning evaporating in the repetition,
while the silence between us stretches,
wavering like heat on a distant road.

the space warps—
a widening ripple where connection once lived,
a soft distortion swallowing the shape of us.
still, we pretend to reach across it,
pretend to hear each other through the fog,
pretend the spark is only hiding
and not already gone.

but in the end, it's just another moment
lost in the blur of our unraveling—
a conversation that dissolves on contact,
a scene that feels half-remembered,
a reality we can no longer fully touch.

v. blur

the boundaries dissolve quietly—
light bending,
voices thinning,
memories turning to static.
i wander through the soft distortion,
where every truth becomes uncertain
and every step
leads further into the unnamed.

v. blur

it isn't such a bad place to end things—
this quiet corner where shadows softly fall,
where the weight of finality becomes
less burden than release.

for what is ending
but a subtle peace,
a closing of the book upon the past,
a chapter that completes the tale
and offers rest from the ceaseless quest for more?

in this dusk, where all the lights grow dim,
we find a solace in the stillness here—
a chance to let the echoes of our lives
dissolve into twilight's calm embrace.

so let this be where the journey stops,
not with regret
but with a quiet grace—
for some endings bring a peace
that striving never could.

v. blur

the world dissolves
at the edges of my sight—
colours melting into one another,
names slipping from their shapes.
nothing holds,
nothing stays,
and i drift through it all
like a thought forgetting itself.

m.d.p

h.f

b.s.n.c

k.c

s.e

c.f.k

k.l.r

a.k.s

w.k

m.m

c.c.c

l.m.h

l.p

x.k

n.a

in the breath
after the last thought
where all beginnings
collapse

in black
we disappear

www.ingramcontent.com/pod-product-compliance
Lightning Source LLC
Chambersburg PA
CBHW061335040426
42444CB00011B/2933